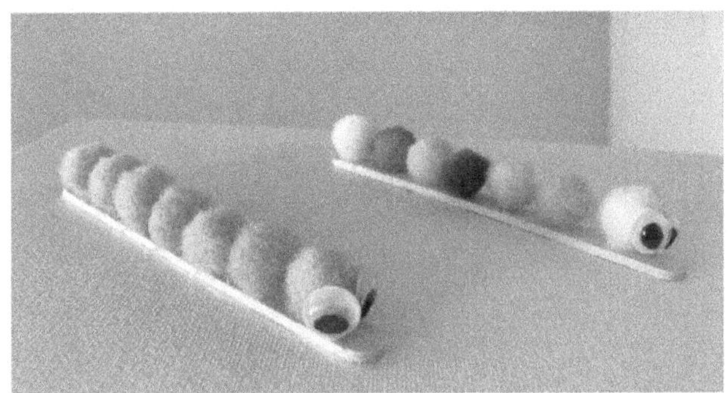

Do Me a Solid

By Refried Bean

Do Me a Solid

By Refried Bean

Acknowledgements

Thank you, Peer workers United, Michelle Dyson, Dan Frey, Tishna Lopez, Chaplain Sandra, Chaplain Michael, Rev Phillip Fleming, Mary Alice, Claire Bateman, Marilyn Shipe Beck, Ginger DeMint, Justin Kyle Crolley, Morgan Collins, John Keasler, Janice Robinson, Lynn Thompson, Tracey Haynes, Courtney O'Meally, Daphne, Melissa, Grace, Daniel, Richard, Aleksandra Zukoff, Erik, Joanna, Amy, Trinity Forum, The Preppy Kitchen, Sarah Kain Gutowski, Patricia Raybon, Jane Poirier Hart, Lyle Schmerz, Betsy Miller, Miller Junior, Scott and Heather Nelson, Abby Cooler, Whitney Bryant, Shambryln, Dr. Avitabile, Dr. Sacco, Dr. Goyal, Barbara Lock, Hannah Park, Jeanna Maloney, Rebecca Yager, Paige O'Shields, Erin Coker, Robert Vivian, Dr. Michael Lindsey, Allison Vrbova, Howard, Louis Taylor, Juanita Edwards, Greg Hill, Stephanie Taylor, Genevieve Rand, Nadia Abadir, Sue from Barnes and Noble, Andrew, Shannon from Con Edison, Kali Van white bal, Jessica Gilbert, Kate Senecal, Jenn and Keith Cevasco, Mickie Belcher, Sherrie Templeton, Joanna Smyers, Jennifer Davis, Tomoko Takahama, Stefanie and Zach, Jamie Magnum, Eve Otten, Erin Haithcock, Supal Desai, Mrs. Toney, Michelle, Mike Jackson, Antoinetta Contreres, Elinor Greenberg, David Mc Phee, Richard, The Beckfords, Kim Jolly, Angel Jolly, Mr. Jolly, Debby Jolly, Rosemary Hayes, Jared Chesson, Jamie Albert, Jennifer Adamson, Andrea Mathers, Alicia Mathers, Ina Garten, Dr. Cotes, Macy's, Beef Jerky Store, Stephanie Ludlum, Amy Roper, Lori Greenberg, Gap, Shannon Whitehouse Klocko, Michele Labar, Jennifer Gough, Andy Croston, Thomas, Amy the Methodist, Tishna, Montez, Chris Hastings, Lauren, Christopher Huber, Davy, Charles P, Joseph Soto, Bernard Chang, Heather, Stephanie Geter Young, Adouwa, Uzunmba, McMahon, Karen Bo Lee, Erdman Center, John, Joy, Byron, HP, Anthony, Candace, Ebony, Garrett, Tanelia, Jack, Neil Guterman, Margarita Mooney Suarez, Monnie Whitson, Grace, Camila De Vasconselos, Falguni, Chibarros, Kimberly, Monique, Alex, Melissa, Sophia Lin, Scala Foundation, Princeton Theological Seminary, Sean Barnette, Grace, Dr. Desai, Diego, Alice Rochester, Holland Varn, Kate, Niki Stonebreaker Neems, Kelly Mc., Jill, The Preppy Kitchen, Claire, Kalen, Takisha Cannon, Brad Rollins, Donna Lazar, Echo Church, Rick and Kay Warren, Zach and Jillian, Dr. Owens, Myron Brown,

Genghis Khan, Mrs. Leslie, Mr. Freeman, Richard, Brian, Frances, Kenny, Tanka, Elyse, Natoya, Germaine, Adam, Chen Chen, Lucia Galloway, Anna Gergen, Karen Greenbaum-Maya, Carla Sameth, Neema Ejercito, Sapreet, Victoria Lin, Avi Nocella, Ji Yong Kim, UJA, Montefiore, Alyssa Janof, Edith Katz, Faith Gateway, Ann Voskamp, Margaret Feinberg, Ann Cardinal, Louise Crowley, Bret Lott, Stephen King, Barbara Ehrenreich, Amy Tan, Barbara Kingsolver, Barnes and Noble customers from 2558, Patti, Mrs. Hellman, Mrs. Leech, Mrs. Richmond, Mrs. Pike, Mrs. Hadden, Mrs. Oney, Mr. Garrett, X files, Matt Groening, Sesame Street, Portfolio Center, Jim Henson Productions, Jill Evans, John, Tracy Benjamin, Tai Little, Claire G, Hector, Dee Brian, Maxie, Andy the Comedian, Lynn Carlson, Ayako Lino, Neil, Bookstore Margaret, Jax, Sam and Georgie, Kelly McConnell, Bethanie Henderson, Lea Pescora, Tia DesJardins, Rose Chaney, Shane Claiborne, Alana Saltz, Scabigail, Alton Brown, etc, Greg Silverman, Stephen Yee, Michelle Gann, Minda Shelton, Pendleton Place, Melanie, Anna, Hannah, Vineyard Vines, RL Polo, Old Navy, Simple, Hanes, Nike, Adidas, Wal-Mart, Fresh Market, Whole Foods, Spinx, Earthfare, Chick-fil-A, QT Station, Joy Food, Charlie's Barbecue, Chipotle, India Palace, Monterrey's, Corona's, Carrabas, Spill the Beans, City Range, Kanpai of Tokyo, Grand China Buffet, Alex, Jacob, and Amy Sherbert, Rvnt, Alexandria Ocasio-Cortez, Migel, Pedro, Lopez, Shay Black, Gilbert Kalu, Makila Meyers, Jeniffer Minaya, Renee, Walter, Frank, Isabel, Mr. Jordan, DDG, Ronelle, Michael, Peaches, Silvette, Gladys, Brian, Azazuma, Chakeezee, New Guy, Ugly Volvo, Acknowledgments of the Unknown Conspirators, Starbucks people, Car people, MTA bus drivers, Subway people, train 6 stations, Bellevue, Jacobi, NYU, New York Presbyterian Virtual Care, Mt. Sinai, CVS Greenville, Gables at Pelham, Rolling Green Assisted Living, Sears, Kmart, Tanzania Church, Sheryl Sandberg, Instagram, Meta, Saffy the Spaniel, Blanket Sea, Julia, Kamala Harris, Hello Humans, Skeeter Powell, Johnny Price, Mitchell and Catherine Poe, Jennifer Grant, David Hogg, The Onion, The Dodo, Nadia Bolz-Weber, Amanda Freitag, Malala, Serena Williams, Venus Williams, Lisa Crayton, Sue Ganz-Scmitt, Amadou, Demba, Glenys Nellist, Anne Elrod Whitney, Alicia Bee, Tara62, Lady Patriot, Butters Kennedy, Igor, Daschund Heaven, Barney, Sir Tobias Waddlesworth, Laura Dorwart, Donald Quist, Joshua Hager, Andrew McG, Flypaper Guy, Blood Buddy, Thister.

poems

God knows that trick

when the grocery store is collecting pop tarts
for the homeless shelter,
don't say,
"I wish I was poor."
Just buy yourself some pop tarts some time
and try to keep a job.

At church, don't make fun of that lady
with the head tremor
by pretending you have a head tremor.
Just nod a little bit when the preacher says
something about Jesus.

I mean, my Gosh,

not everyone can work in a Tic Tac factory
and watch movies about rodents
on their lunch break.
If you want gallbladder surgery,
then damage your gallbladder.
It all adds up if you multiply by eleven.

10 thousand odes to groundhogs

My history is not everyone's history.

It could be a good idea

To scrog a groundhog on video

In case you are ever accused of child abuse

And you can say,

Clearly I like groundhogs.

I says, my friend,

This could be enough in the genre,

And you don't know

What some groundhogs

Have been through.

What if this is the only poem someone ever reads?

I should make the lines all rhyme

To have the poem be worth their time.

And then do something really nice

By saying how to cook some rice

Which means you boil it in a pot

And cook ten minutes while it's hot.

But that is still not great enough

For one dear poem in life so rough

So just in case you're still alive

My debit pin's 5555.

Pizza for One

God is treating himself
To some correct regard in my mind today.
Some perception of him as a nice God.
A good giver who cares about my life.
A creative director who thought of some
funny mental health adventures.
Some life that I had a say in or didn't,
As I also treat myself to a frozen pizza,
Which was just what God knew I wanted.

Poem

I think something
people would not expect
Is if bomber planes
dropped a bunch of
ploughshares on a country.

Do you find this funny?

I'm like a troubled teen,
Except a grownup.

Episodic

In heaven,

Jesus Christ will probably have his own TV show.

And you know what kind of show I bet it will be?

A religious show. Something about religion.

People say no not necessarily

But sometimes things are predictable,

such as the next trillion years,

the next trillion songs,

the next trillion meals,

and this ad for the Jesus Show.

Poem

What should we do for the next generation?

Let's outlaw friendship,

Just as a surprise,

Like something the other generations didn't think of,

Or at least as much.

This too shall pass

Do you know what I think is over-reacting?
When you have an awkward moment
And you think,
"This too shall pass."

God saved my disgusting family from their sin

My dad's rude belching.
My mom's dirty feet.
My sister's botched facelift.
My own bloody pads
Stenching up everyone's lives.
We should have thrown ourselves in the garbage dump
When I was in kindergarten.
No one is who they should have been.
Everyone's winning sperm
should have been more polite and deferred.
That is original sin, way before conception,
For people to not even exist as themselves.
We can't possibly be real,
and in heaven we will find out our true race,
human or not.
No one exists unless we all do.
Don't think Australia is innocent.
If Mary is a magic goose
Then I can be a muppet.
Why do you have to be told this?
It was already encoded in your nails.

Explanation

Because of hell, anything can be holy.
Because of christ, you can be holy
without going to hell.

Anger in the hands of a sinner's God

They say we hang by just a thread
But that will sometimes cause me dread
When people need salvation fast
And I am scared they will not last

I feel the pressure for their case
And think the thread is my own face
And anything I say and do
Is how God chooses who is who.

With stuff all hinging on my life
And what I say to solve their strife
So then they tell me their demands
That cause me shackles, traps and bands

But that is simply not my job
To say who has to wail and sob
So next time I'll refer them where
Our God will let me just not care.

Jesus is the mourning star

Jesus rises in the east
Or in the west or where its best
Or where its worst or where its first
Or where there's people who are cursed.

He spins the worlds that heaven holds
And heals the cruelest winter colds
And tells the darkness it must hide
And says he knows that people lied

He takes the poems that have no truth
And writes them in the book of ruth
And takes the art that shouldn't be
And makes a better mystery.

He says I know you didn't care
Except your heart is truly there
And that is why the angels fly
In God's own glory of the sky.

Hell-o patients

When I am dying in a hospital some day

I am not going to pull the fire alarm in the hallway
 just as a final prank and childhood wish granted.

It's just not considerate

And why make everyone run from a fake fire

when there's a real one they could be saved from now

Fragment

Picking up the mustard and ketchup
For a memorial day barbecue,
lest we forget.

What's for Lunch

If you say
"a rare hamburger"
Do you mean
You don't eat meat that much,
Or that it is not well done.

That's not the kind of sloth I am

Our Bible lesson today
Is that everything you do hurts Jesus Christ.

Joking.

Joking of course,

this joke is on page 59 of the Living Bible.

Turn with me if you will

to the middle of your pot luck cookbook.

The recipe is for what you should have cooked

Each day instead of what you did cook

Or order, or eat in the restaurant,

Or say and do instead of what
God now has to work with,

Which actually is pretty good material, isn't it,

At least for the persecutors,

Or the people now listed

In the Book of Strife

The Book of Life

The book of Abraham's knife,

Lot's Wife,

salvation for all mankind

except the people

who bother us.

Seventh Grade

God said,

Let us fashion together

A rude person.

Someone made of twizzle sticks and candy wrappers,

Ten trillion light years of stardust,
Plus some bad habits and an attitude
That says, I will ask Jesus for sarcasm
as my birthday present this year.

What can be mocked if not
The faces of all friends to be had,
To be seen or complimented
On ways that don't offend
Or at least in the same way
As all my other friends
For anything they say and do
Unless they help me laugh
At everyone else
As we eat pie
and break the mirrors
in the funhouse
called school.

Legal Statement

Anyone reading this safety blurb implicitly agrees to enter a contract of future obligation to work one year in the insult factory of heaven's questionable probation chamber. Salaries will be based on hilarity tolerance for prank chair announcements totaling one fifth of the amount decided by forty panels of people found connected to the incidents in question from hearsay. This notice is enforced by the mystery district of withheld criticism during the times later noted for more people's entertainment in either a safe or funnier location. Odd wondering and mental revisits or dismissal and denial constitute a legally binding signature on all views likely.

Mad Lib Poem

_______________ and yet _______________ because
____

____

_______________ ___________ _____________

However _________________

___________ _______________ _______________

But what I find most inappropriate and offensive is

_____________ ___________________________

____

_______________.

Please don't tell anyone that _________________
____

___________________ _____________

Or about my criminal behavior described in my journal.

They should name schizophrenia

Something more easy to understand

Like Scramble brain

Or Odd Thought Disease

Or Jolt-a-mind

Or Lurchawhirl

Or What's that noise

Or wow who do you think you are

To write such an offensive poem

About something so horrible

As Horrible Nightmare Disorder.

And I will say, that is the point,

Is that I think I'm so important

That it is up to me

To tell everyone

They have

"A-lot-of-nerve."

Blog Posts

Failed Evangelism as Predestination

Ok, should I say Evangelicalism? Not everything is about problems in my own time and country. But this is an interesting theological topic that has to do with people's rejection of the gospel of Jesus Christ, or maybe the church's failure to present the true gospel that is by nature "irresistible." So here we go, this is presbyterian theology. The idea is this: the great commission that Jesus gave his disciples after a total defeat of all death and his own acceptance of all authority in heaven and earth says "Go make disciples of all men." *All* men, and yet any thorough survey of the bible would at least call into question most "lapses" into universalism. On some eternal level, most Christians believe that there end up being saints and aints. That's actually not something I am questioning that much in this post, though sometimes I do try to think of how some people might like being in hell. But what I am wondering about is whether people's personal failure and even all too fast giving up on sharing their faith is not just one of God's tools for destiny but actually his main strategy for choosing who will be redeemed. And that the most human aspect of it, which can even in totality be seen as personal achievement or failure, might be exactly proportionally the most key factor in predestination. I say that based on the great commission only, though verses like John 3:16 might also be relevant. This idea that salvation really was meant for everyone, and that the task of sharing the gospel was left to humans in some way, could mean that gaining converts might be an equal blessing to losing converts. And that by not succeeding and experiencing ever increasing grief over the loss of the world could be a way of joining God in his rejection which was the inevitable manifestation of his loving nature on the cross. The jealous God of the Old Testament, a father who gave his own son to a world that hurt him, the son who was despised and rejected, and the holy spirit with a loss that can't be told. What better honor could there be than to see everyone you care about choose hell over listening to what you have to say.

A Concept Called Righteousness Privilege

Hi everyone, I'm putting this topic on my theology blog though it could go on my mental health blog. It is a topic that I have a delayed idea of but have been aware of twice in academic contexts where it really would have been valuable to share. And the concept is basically something called "righteousness privilege." At social work school, our textbook mentioned "Christian privilege," and I didn't appreciate it and saw it mostly as an anti-religious bias. Later, in a short certificate program about medieval Christianity, I said I sometimes felt like monks were privileged. But I partially forgot about the real reasons I have for feeling that way, which mostly aren't financial, like a lot of privilege is, but it has to do with good deeds and kindness and the circumstances that allow you to successfully keep your own moral standards and follow Jesus Christ in an effective way. Not everyone is remotely allowed to be at their best and serve others how they would want to or might if they were taught better. I actually think that this could be a whole book and I could write about forty pages on it right now. But this blog is not like that and I also don't even want to do a three page rant like what is currently on my regular blog. I just want to introduce the concept and say that within all the overlapping economies of poverty and wealth, that there is this other thing that people dearly want called being good, which can also be a form of beauty. And that on some levels it can be bought or earned, but on many levels, it can't, and that the way Jesus Christ made the real thing not just available to anyone but actually only available through his own sacrifice is the core gift of Christianity. It is a costly justice that in all cases is also merciful and withstands any worldly accusations of favoritism or just plain falseness. The relevant fact is that what God for us did was so precious and undeserved by anyone that you don't call it privilege and complain when other people have it. You ask for it yourself and then try to have some sign of it in your own life among whatever corruption there also is, whether it is just a few prideful thoughts in a very righteous life, or even the sin by negation where you let yourself be good without caring about other people being bad from either oppression or ignorance.

I don't know if I should add to this now but another thing to consider is situations where some people are deriving their goodness in a system where their value is based on maintaining other people's lack of righteousness in comparison. Think evangelism, jail settings, school and volunteering, or client work of any kind. Also, people who didn't bother to help anyone at all sometimes feel clean in comparison to those who find themselves with some unfair leverage. To me, this is an interesting topic where some of the true traction of power and persecution discussions are. And I know that it was not fair for this to be out of reach in social work school, and that very justice withheld is exactly what is hidden when people suppress the truth of Christian religion.

A large country called Reality

This is a post I have been meaning to write for a while on a topic that obviously calls for further thought. Partially it is a correction and realization of something I mentioned in a paper I wrote for a school program. In the paper, I was writing about why Jewish people are so often persecuted, and that is not a light topic. I am not talking about people getting a bad grade unfairly or being uninvited to parties. I am of course referencing things like mass murder and the holocaust. So anyway I said it was because of both race and religion, but after being in a habit now for a while of thinking of things in threes, I see that there is a third identity factor for a whole people and that is the concept of "nation." So it is race, religion, and nation. And currently Israel has a chunk taken out of it called Palestine which is officially recognized on some maps and supported by many political people from other know-it-all places like some of the United States. I don't know what will happen with all of that. I personally support extending Israel's borders into Syria and Iraq to create a safe zone with new rules and culture in the middle east. But anyway I mention that also because I think that the "race, religion, nation," identity combo for populations is also relevant to why people want Christian nationalism in the United States. It was something that did exist more organically for a while but was lost. But part of what that Christian nation tried to provide was another trio called "liberty and justice 'for all.'" "For all" is the third part of another set of three things. It really is a helpful thing to look for those trilogy combos, and something that people used to do more when some amount of Christian education was the standard for most thought. That too, was lost, and there will be a cost to it, though I am in the camp that sees a lot of it as sacrificial outreach that will reap a good harvest of inclusion instead of total destruction. But anyway, that "liberty and justice for all" trinity had a different mission than just forcing everyone to subscribe to the main religion, and religious liberty was something that people did try to offer as a nation, and actually succeeded with in some ways. And people who want to fight that are having to in some ways make their aggressive politics turn into a new religion itself, which I believe will be exponentially a worse embarrassment than pipe dreams of Christian nationalism. This post is kind of political to put on my theology blog, but notice the concepts. It is very theological and these principles will not be skipped or ignored successfully by anyone.

What Does It All Mean

Ok everyone, this is just another correction of something I have said before, though I think I should be able to use hyperbole in a rant to make a point. But anyway I recently said that Christianity was the only true religion, and I mostly do believe that, but want to point out that actual, accurate Christianity is actually Judeo-Christianity. And people have often talked about "Judeo-Christian" values, and the success that happens when people like Jews and Christians work together. But I want to say that just plain Christianity by itself is inherently "Judeo-Christian." So what some people are talking about is actually "Judeo-Judeo Christian." It has to do with why the Old Testament is part of the Bible, and totally legit and not lesser. So anyway, there are theological discussions of what all can count as "Judaism" and someone's personal "old testament" in their life or religion or historical background. It is very interesting and also has to do with systems of mercy and justice. So I just wanted to mention that on my theology blog because I think a lot of Christians and maybe even most of us have not thought of Christianity as being already "Judeo-Christian." All people say is "hey, Jesus was Jewish," but that gets old, and one of the reasons it does is because all of reality is relevant to the discussion, not just one guy's bloodline.

Offense and Defense

Ok everyone, here is another actual question I have on my theology blog instead of just an opinion or something I have learned. It has to do with "isms," and when legitimate religion turns into a problem "ism," and a sort of idolatry problem. That was what happened with Catholicism on such a mass scale that the Reformation happened and some Christians started a new branch of Christianity without ever looking back. The religion had folded in on itself and people were no longer freely worshipping God but entangled by idolatry and self-justification of all sorts. Much later on, in our country, some geniuses eventually coined the term "fundamentalism," and suggested that the same thing was happening with Protestantism, only it was the skeletal basics of Christianity that had become the new distraction from God himself.

I personally, in both cases, think that the fact that actual Jesus is involved and is prayed to in each belief system, offers supernatural protection from total loss, and that it is most likely that the religion itself and especially God's goodness will still win out and benefit individuals and society. However, it is a very interesting topic, and bad stuff does happen in God's name all the time from all of it. It is a very common type of "taking God's name in vain," though most people associate that with more instant sins of saying G- dm and OMG.

So anyway, this brings me to my theological question, which is whether than can be something like "Jesus-ism" or God-ism, as well, where an actual truth-based relationship with God can also become some kind of barrier to health and life. And I think maybe the answer is possibly, in some ways, but mostly that is the point of why you worship God with no other Gods before him, is because he has the infinitude to absorb worship without anything bouncing back to harm people. So that if you can weave through those other corruptible mazes, you do hit something that delivers and by nature and definition protects you from the Ism Idolatries.

This is also why I don't support witch hunts against fundamentalists. It is just too likely that despite any amount of intellectual or cultural poverty, some of those prayers will be real and answered in ways that tap into all the resources and truth that exist.

A Rather Extreme View itself

Ok everyone, here is another blog post for the mad blog which is more reflective and less mad this time. And it has to do with political "extremism" often being seen as a key problem or even the key problem on either "side," when really it's not always a difference in degree and devotion behind the most damaging people. Those who tear up society shouldn't be automatically seen as just hyper-motivated versions of normal people, or over-involved ideology representatives who somehow got carried away with what would have been a good cause. Truly detrimental views and actions often have a totally different orientation towards some kind of wrong living. Problem people who political campaigners want to associate with their opponents have a variety of motives and bad belief systems. This is one of the reasons why it's not working out for people to reduce everything to a dual political party fight in the first place, which millions have in fact fallen for. But even those who cast a vote of any kind don't necessarily subscribe and oppose in the patterns that so many activists and politicians would want to make it seem. So how much more so are the crazy criminals not just some kind of highly concentrated form of legitimate mainstream directions. There is such thing as extremism, there is such thing as going off the deep end, but I am tired of people saying that bad people are just me but worse, or me, but "more so." Or me, but more progressed along the exact path I am on, which is doing the best I can like most other people. Do people really want everything to be about politics? To be decided by one check mark on a piece of paper every four years? The people who want that must not have any

other deeds to their name. I feel sorry for them and for
everyone who has to live in the same country as them.

The Guns Are Pointed At The Wrong People

I'm a little late with this and truly sorry about that, but I have some thoughts about how AR -15s are in fact way past what is appropriate for civilian availability and should certainly not be given to people who have already proven themselves as not even being "civil." But also in terms of what is civil and what is war, there is something else I have to add to the gun debate which is that I think for all the shootings there are at least that many people who should have been shot instead. The death penalty could and should also be part of this discussion of mass shootings, as well as the fact that 30 thousand dollars a year gets spent on facilitating jail for murderers who took innocent lives and don't deserve to live. That is also part of a picture where disabled people are given a third of minimum wage to live on when instead they should have been included in the work force, which is also widely underpaid. All of these problems are related to valuing and not valuing life, which should generally be protected "to the death." Some people like to say, "Who are we to choose who can live" when they pretend to be moral and above the death penalty instead of beneath it. But actually, for centuries, people have quite often been moral enough to make that call, and they will do so again if and when there is war because of these unresolved problems. The immorality and amorality and cowardice of those who do not stand up to crime is absolutely part of this same problem, and don't think that is not a major factor in why up to half the country refuses to give up access to what are clearly very dangerous and very modern weapons meant for legitimate military protection.

Media Outlets

ok, everyone here is another mad blog topic which has to do with publishing. And that is the transformation of the meaning of "platform" in recent years. I could be wrong but I think that "platform" used to refer more to a perspective and background of an author, sometimes even including their story communicated in their work itself. Now, in some circles, the term is used almost interchangeably with "following," referring to contacts on facebook or twitter, etc. I agree that some overlap makes sense and is simply a fact, but mostly I think this conflation reflects slight cheating from the publishing industry, who wants it to go unnoticed that the author has to supply their own publicity now, as well as an aggression from other influencers who see their political and social advantage and want to equate the author's worth and meaning with popularity.

This leap of reference and the expectation that everyone will go along with it and either won't notice the difference, won't acknowledge the change, or just never knew until they were taught this new view of things, has implications that I think could go beyond the impact of books and communication, on into philosophical and religious grounding within this culture and others. It's just a step in a selling-out process, and could be more dangerous than people realize when truth is up for a vote and majority mob rule has the last word. And that itself is the deception, because it's not even a matter of having the last word, but a claim that the popularity is the word itself. Go ahead and stretch that interpretation all the way to people thinking they're God. It's not far from the tragedy of a whole industry and profession agreeing on that shortcut together.

People can say, oh, selling out, like how your books
haven't sold out so you're complaining. Maybe, but I
don't know who can read them anyway if people are
just going to change the definitions of words and
exchange prophets for profits.

The Powers That Were

Well everyone, this is not really a whole blog post but
just a sketch for a post. It has to do with powers that
be. And just that I remember as a kid sometimes my
dad or someone would point out something interesting
about a product, or a store, or the way things were
done, and say an explanation like "they do that because
of such and such." They have the label on the side so you
won't get mixed up with whatever." The railing is like
this because such and such. And a lot of times it would
be something logical and protective. Like plastic bags
being labeled for safety. Then, in the late nineties,
someone said something like, "at Bilo they pump a
bread smell into the air so people will buy more." And
this was different than some kind of strategy to help
people. It was about the cash. And I guess a lot of stuff
was always about the cash, but I think that things have
gotten even worse now, where it's not even about the
cash. It is about power, also because of cash, but also
just for the power. Products being unsafe, ingredients
not being labeled, power plays, cash register lines with
not enough cashiers, music that is too loud, music that is
inappropriate, credit card devices that threaten refusal
to serve, etc. Honestly I don't have great examples for
any of it. That is why I say it is not even a whole blog
post, much less an article. But I know I am right. And a
lot of the people who won't acknowledge this decline
(get it, declined, like your credit card when you don't
match a profile) anyway, I am saying a lot of people who
are in denial think they are the ones who are going to be
at an advantage as people set up these bad systems, but
I think everyone is going to suffer. Even the ones
getting the profit will not have the joy of living in a fair
society. It won't benefit them either in the long run. It's

just something I noticed, something that almost seems the same and is probably used to criticize some people who suggest that there has been loss as well as gain in recent decades. But it is a sign for the logical reasons for things to not be in our favor anymore, in this evil "our."

Expect Betrayal From The Social Work Schools

A lot of insurance dollars come from DSM classifications for mental disorders but many social work schools are well into a transition from their once life-saving medical support to a new stance of tearing up thousands of people's mental health as their altered mission of so called racial justice. Some of it is kind of obvious but when you are actually in social work school it can be slow to dawn on you. You just think that everyone would be there to help people but there is a "white fragility" narrative that includes unexpected rejoicing at the one in four mental health crisis and even better than that, increasing rates of autism behind a lot of the new white poverty. But white poverty is actually not discussed that much as the people barking at you to not touch their hair literally are petted like animals by the liberal curriculum and then sicced like dogs onto conservatives. I wouldn't go for it myself, but promoting anti-white racism is actually one of the main recruitment strategies to attract the diverse student population they are so proud of, so some perspectives are already established beforehand and then reinforced with the tuition money of people who don't get scholarships for assuming everyone else is biased. How much detail would be good to share in a post like this? In a way, despite all the obscure reference citations and dense articles in an out-of-reach curriculum, it's not that complicated. It is middle school level harassment. But when you are there, you can't help but believe some of what they teach, and it is normal to suspect yourself of being racist as you risk your life every day to go to internships in dangerous neighborhoods full of the now government funded drug dealers and child abusers. However, the lies eventually wear off and you figure out that it's not so much that you are racist, per se, but that you are white... and they are racist. "Ha ha," all the people who aren't reading this blog say. "This is exactly what we were trying to tell you." But unfortunately, resentment like this is exactly what I paid for when I earned the 80-thousand-dollar dirty buddhism license that I can't ever use because my social work school taught my whole city to discriminate against me on the basis of... everything about me.

No Can't Do, Mr. McFeely

Spectrums have become popular in recent times to explain complicated things, especially mental disorders involving a 3D wrinkled blob of jello. I actually think it's not that useful of a construct, even for autism and especially for bipolar disorder, which already had a good name of "manic depression." Kay Redfield Jameson was by far the leading scholar and published a huge encyclopedia by that name, but almost exactly after she did, rich white child abusing doctors who had not yet discovered opioid drug dealing opportunities started peddling a new name of "bipolar disorder." Of course it seemed like genius, since happy is simply the exact opposite of sad, isn't it? I mean, some people don't learn that until they are four years old. But anyway, I just want to add another spectrum to the mix, which I think sometimes really is measurable by degrees, and that is the "I don't care" / "I can't care" spectrum. It has to do with people only being able to take so much, and how some people's "don't seem to care" is really a matter of having cared so much that they maxed out. And there is simply nothing left. I'm not suggesting that everyone start saying "I can't care," when they can't come through on whatever the next demand is for their attention, because I think that can still hurt the people needing help. But when people are assessing how much to blame themselves for certain limits of strength and heart, then it might be useful for them to know themselves that their feeling of not caring enough actually might have a mix of "can't" in it, and they might be the ones in need.

We are the champions, my friend.

Hi everyone, here are some photos of my old class jersey from the Eastside Week reverse gender football game. Refried Bean is a nickname I have had since middle school. Now it is my pen name on the books I have been publishing since 2016. Possibly my books will be challenged, or my pen name, or some other kind of legal harrassment. But I am innocent and honest and if you don't support someone like me then you are not a real social justice advocate or a true evangelical. I hope you all enjoy the books. I expect to be harrassed and abused for the rest of my life that probably only has about five years left. There seems to already be a line of people waiting to do lawsuits but all of them are bad people who should have waited to see what I could have personally given them if I had not been censored and pre-crime m

Fathoming and Forgetting

Well everyone, I hope you are having a nice day. I am doing okay and my apartment is about to be inspected at my supported housing program for mental illness. I have been busy for a few days and attended a prayer conference this past weekend. I always see visions when I participate in programs and classes from the seminary that hosted the event, and sure enough, I saw several days of prophecy and hallucinations and experiences of the Bible seeming lit up for me. It was great and the people were really nice to include me. I think some bad things got wrangled and my prayers will continue to be powerful despite some mental decline.

I am signed up for another conference that is much different this weekend at the same place. There has been some possibility of not being able to handle it but I think I will be fine and it has a good overlap with art in the world so it is not just pure monk power that will send me off the deep end. Here is an article that I think describes my conditions well, though at the core of it I feel like I have been confronting the war against my soul and all souls as described in the whole book of 1 Peter. I like Peter and associated him with Catholicism but his opening paragraph in that book is very Presbyterian. The article:

www.ncbi.nlm.nih.gov/pmc/articles/PMC5613459/

This blog has a lot of posts written while being gutwrenched to the point of organ damage and irreversible mental deterioration, and I have to say that when I see the heart of it in religious settings, I agree with myself that some of it is from injustice that is not my fault. There is opportunity in it to worship and be blessed without dependence on exterior affirmation from a failing and falling world, but really, there is no excuse for me to be catapulted into super saint status without bringing the millions of people with me who could have benefited from my normal life and work. I can feel the truth of it when I say that it is wrong, that there is now a ten year crime against me that hurts my whole society and world, and it will only get worse without some kind of reversal and acknowledgement. I keep trying to guess what my next steps are, and it seems that for some reason, there are hundreds of people partaking in the suffering instead of millions of people benefiting from our work. So that is where I will have some trust of a will behind a will, and God's patience with so much more disrespect than I have felt myself. The affront to God needs to be understood before people aspire to reach the nations with his love. Some of his mercy is in the fact that he would care enough to feel the great offense, and I think that learning about this was what took me from a parkinson's dementia problem to renewal of a deeper understanding of God's forgiveness and patience.

The Lord Gives and the Democrats Take Away

Hi everyone, I am in Greenville right now visiting my mom and dad. It is like a captivity situation but I only have seven more days. I survive by being thankful for what is good about it which mostly has to do with comfort and food. I also have a few friends that I am able to socialize with, though the main problem is that I can't socialize well because I do not have a car. And really I could borrow my dad's truck, but my mom would freak out. And that is the main issue is that my mom controls me irrationally and emotionally punishes me no matter what I do. So if I use a certain plate or bowl then we might have twenty conversations where I justify my decision. It is actually I think beyond anything that people can understand in this life and I just have to believe that God understands and that someday it will be over.

My dad is living in assisted living now and I thought he was safe there but he fell last night because they are not that vigilant about keeping him safe. But he is not supposed to get up by himself but the fact is that he did and it is their job to keep him from falling. So that is unreliable but I think I will advise my mom to just keep him there and know there is nothing that we can do about how people treat us. People are mean to me in New York, too, and there are multiple networks of people who target me personally with their racism and harrassment. And yet I see our country being ruined too and know that it could be an entire generation of young people who have it worse in our country full of about two thirds savage barbarians. So I will just keep staying alive, praying, and waiting until someone goes too far.

This blog is ruined. You can tell I tried to share my faith
but that is not really the whole issue. At first my writing
was just friendly high quality and it wasn't that
religious. But people have reduced my life to only
having hope for heaven, so that is what I try to share
with other people. But it doesn't matter does it. I simply
have no online outlet for good communication
anymore. Facebook took themselves back. I kind of feel
sorry for them because it could have been a historical
legacy lasting hundreds of years but they chose the
politics or the money or something that ruined one of
the best things that ever happened to people. They are
like billionaire failures. Another interesting thing is how
nerdy some of this persecution is. Like it is the history
nerds from school who want to be in the textbooks
seeming like latin revolutionaries or whatever else they
saw in their school lessons other than the baby killers
that they are. Happy Mothers Day, we're coming for
your tax dollars to kill everyone's full term children.
Self-righteousness without the righteousness. The finale
to four year of relentless political abuse is Biden
stuttering in Poland as China and Iran prepare to come
take slaves from America. I could literally keep writing
for twenty more pages about the same stuff that
depresses me every day. But in some ways, it just isn't
necessary, because EVERYONE ALREADY KNOWS.
That's why you are censoring us. Because you don't
want the truth to be told. But everyone already knows
it and you have recorded yourselves deliberately
ruining the lives of almost the whole world for multiple
generations. We all know what you did and how fake
your protests are and how you have to call anyone who
does what they are supposed to a supremacist to try to
explain the growing difference between the socialist

hell holes and the flourishing grocery economies of the places where people chose service instead of empty, abusive activism.

A pinata for the Democratic Party

That is what I am in New York City. A target for people's hypocritical bullying. Some people have it worse and can't go to the grocery store at all. But I am almost there myself and receive a psychological punishment for almost anything I do, which was also how my family problems were that I have still not escaped from despite moving far away and funding my own existence with borrowed money, some of which is from other people who are treated the same way. How long will that be maintained. I will tell you that I think not much longer, and that eventually the good pinatas like me will run out and you will be hitting things with shards of glass and nails flying into your blind racist eyes.

How to go down in history:

This flag did not persecute me:

This flag does persecute me:

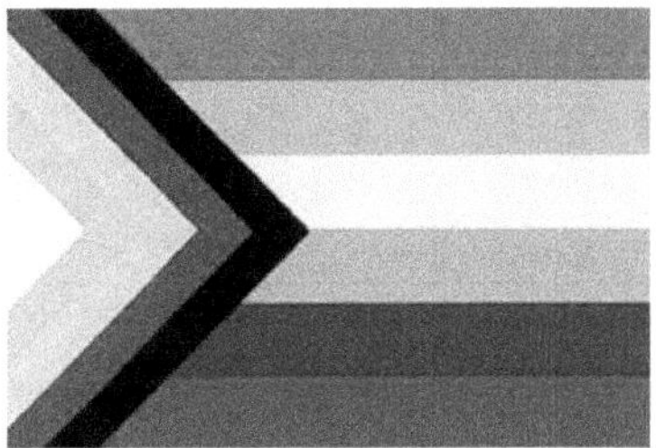

There are a variety of intents among a diverse group of people with different experiences, speaking of diversity. But generally, I will say that to me, the rainbow flag was a relevant symbol of brave people sticking up for themselves, and the newer, complicated flag is a flag of control freaks who got greedy. Conflators who wanted revenge and domination, and stolen fame in front of some imagined history that is destroying its own audience on purpose, including young people suffering with real gender differences. I will be working out my disgust from this persecution for the rest of my life.

Hate is what they want from me and what their flag stands for. People can say what they mean and don't mean, but the truth is often more apparent than what people will admit, and hundreds of millions of people who were betrayed by the same hypocrits know exactly what I am talking about. Believe me or don't believe me, and support me or don't. The truth will be known and play itself "out."

What you want from Your Hair is Not There

Identity politics is failing. Here in New York, people will soon have to either violate or repeal civil rights laws to get away with how they are treating people. People will have to overtly block the food supply like the murderers in Darfur, and any pretense of civilization will be gone. The work spent to get other people's paychecks could always have been actual economic progress instead, with a harvest that now will not happen. You can't have it both ways, and the fact is that to keep the power you chose instead of justice you have had to join with a forty year assault on the people who did what they were supposed to. The north made its choice to teach everyone that people could do and believe anything with no consequences, and now on a deadly level the lack of goodwill problem-solving has cost our country both safety and liberty. People think no one has noticed the little leaps in logic, the little cheatings in philosophy, and the way political traitors have held the door open for rapists and murderers. But everyone has eyes, good or bad. You can't take away the righteousness that has happened from people who trust in God and do what he says. No one is perfect, but a basic orientation to what is right and good will show itself, and anyone who has devoted even the slightest allegiance to actual justice sees liberal hypocrisy for what it is. Our disgust is as accurate as your outrage is fake. The audience for your charade is disappearing, and everyone knows how bad you must have been for whitey and the man to end up as Ghandi in this scenario.

Downfall of Blog and Country

Well everyone, can I ever return to my blog as just a fun journal instead of a list of all-encompassing grievances of which there is no limit for more material?

I think some stuff has happened that makes it too late for people to benefit from what I have to say. Possibly some of my poetry books will get to the next people and be good for entertainment and small scale religious support. But a bad cloud of politics definitely had its way over my very decent and legitimate attempts to participate well in mass communication.

So the idea to share for this post is that I think our country should consider breaking up, though it could be too late for that. Maybe into three countries, maybe North America into some new states with Mexico included as well. Maybe some states combined into provinces like Canada. This could have been done through treaties, laws, and votes, but probably now any solutions like that will not be peaceful. Political people just were too intent on having their way and they were media people, so they ate up our facebook free speech blessing and will now weild our own friendships as one of their most aggressive weapons. And yet I think there are a lot of people like me who have had enough. There were some late comers to the more liberal views about insurance and gender, and a lot of those people still have a goodness about them that could have been for the whole country. But the less peaceful minded people wanted something other than the justice they claimed to fight for. They wanted to be in the history books defeating their imaginary oppressors. The anti-christianity among so much of it is to me the sign that it won't yield good results and some stuff is probably going to happen to change things in ways people would not expect.

I guess there could be a world war soon, but I also see that a lot of people might have to flee persecution in the United States, and either establish their own territories ungoverned by democratic power freaks, or immigrate to other places like Africa and China with colonial intentions like the Mexicans.

Obviously I am just writing without knowing that much, but there are some things I do know about what will not fly in this world and in God's sight.

Demising and Despising

Well everyone, I hope you are having a good day and don't mind this variety of rant quality complaining on my blog. I really only have a few topics left rattling around in my brain. One of those topics has to do with definitely skipping the arrogance parade in New york for the Juneteenth time this year, and being tired of the pronoun police harassing me even though I actually have legitimate gender problems that their appropriation and religious persecution is based on. I would prefer to have used my pen name Refried Bean ten years ago as soon as I came to New York and then sincerely avoid pronouns according to my lifelong gender suffering, but it is exactly those kind of people who shut me down on a level not just of career loss but of worldwide influence loss. But I am learning that the scale of it that makes me despair also makes it be God's concern and not mine, and I might not even have interest to watch my enemies' brains splatter on judgement day.

Second to mention is just another topic I keep not getting around to and that is the likelihood of reparitions for tax dollars eventually taking place some day in a similar way as slavery payback. I actually do side pretty whole heartedly with slavery reparitions and think it is a goal that can and does happen in disguised forms. But some of the reason I can't make my rightful contribution is from the very same racist politics of people who deny so many other types of leeching, abuse, and deliberate societal harm that happens in our world and country from people of any background.

Thirdly, what is happening with these pandemics and shootings? Will people really not whisper the possibility of biological warfare and foreign attacks? I think some of the assault, both as war and defamation, is a delayed reaction to the British Empire and a still embarrassingly reluctant or involuntary admission that people should have more eagerly accepted the gospel that was shared to them two hundred or so years ago. People's edited anti-colonial narratives have to leave out a lot of facts to continue a denial of what seem to be unprecedented martyrdom opportunities for whole countries and continents, which also happen to be too conspicuously inclusive and diverse for their suffering to be viewed only as a delayed retributive punishment of hypocritical oppression. Whoever demands the baton in their contrived drama of overcoming cultural domination hopefully will be just as successful with sharing the only true and enduring faith of righteous people, which is humble and powerful Christianity. In the US, where people won't shut up about how bad the Christians are, or Republicans, or whoever exactly has been listening to hymns in their cars, some of these suspiciously plentiful and strategically timed shootings have a self-destruction component that kind of reminds me of wars from the 1400s. I say that in code because the northerners have taught me to only pretend to speak out about "injustice," (or is it evil), while they consistently hide their complicitness with bad people and exploiters as much as those they bully. Education on nuclear technology is just too much a worthwhile bargain trade for impressive school diversity stats. All this stuff I politely and RIGHTFULLY kept to myself until people made their choices to harass me and ruin my life. And now I will say why I am bothered, and it will be the same in heaven, when time is up, and God

unleashes his very own individualized slurs that
instantly destroy every nation and people who chose
humiliation over humility.

An Out of Control Blogging Maniac

Hi everyone, it's blog-a-thon Friday, I can't hear you....
What's that? You think I've had enough to write? That is
how it does in fact work and the writer's high combined
with my normal reaction to how things are going for me
in my neighborhood puts me almost in the range of just
a normal extreme depression below any standard scale
in the hospitals I can't afford without leaning too
heavily on "the system." And who hasn't secretly
always wanted to be part of "the system." That is what I
have always said all along, and it is on all my personal
statements for all the school programs that I did to try
to earn even a fraction of minimum wage. I said, "I
would like to be part of "the system," and now my
dreams have all come true. Next I am going to say "I just
want a piece of the pie," only it will be literal strawberry
pie that I bake in my supported housing apartment that
I am probably going to lose now because of complaining
about people trying to give me covid, trying to block me
from the elevator, trying to block me from my own
apartment door, and playing music so loud in my ears
that I have to wonder if they did autism research ahead
of time to get the maximum effect added to my already
damaged brain that got hurt from working in a
bookstore. A night club? No. a loud factory? No. A
bookstore. A jackhammer construction job? No. A
bookstore with music that fried my brain because of its
volume and its deliberately violating content, personally
chosen by Marion and Allison who continued working
there after 30 thousand witnesses saw them ruin my life
on purpose. However, the secret messages are saying
the district manager named Chris is also a torture
suspect at this time. I have to say that I don't know on
that one, so there must be other witnesses who have

already turned in their reports. And she must have worked with lawyers and secret shoppers, so maybe we are waiting on a list of several hundred bad people who are also going to face charges and lose their licenses or social work jobs or whatever it is that people use to attack disabled people with autism. Wow, that is some absurd comedy that will probably be hard for any jury to believe. So I guess we can expect another life ruining farce soon enough, but not before I jot down some notes for all my real readers 500 years from now. You gotta hate it when your worst cashier turns out to be a Confucius or Hafiz, or just a regular christian with accurate faith that God and all his angels are using global warming to invent new weather because they know they do not have enough lightning to strike the Barnes and Noble up and ups who so nobley and barnfully chose and distributed everyone's pornography for all those years.

Honestly It Is A Conundrum

Hi everyone, I hope you are having a nice Sunday so far. I am doing great and just got a reward for good behavior. It is a walker that someone left out in the rain. The conspiracy knew that I knew I will need one eventually, but hopefully not too soon. Ok here is where I decide whether to start complaining, and to say I sometimes feel a collective offense that is also representative, lifelong, thorough, final, complete, representative, personal, cruel, discriminatory, insulting, meant for harm, and accusatory. That is how it feels at least and a lot of it at this point has to do with not having a market for my books and not understanding why. And for people to not understand why that is yet another torture experience, now lasting about two years. And I kind of see how okay it is beyond understanding in some ways and that could help me forgive people for not understanding and it also can make me thankful for the physical manifestation of it which could soon include not being able to walk. Because maybe people will understand or at least believe the impact of chronic emotional abuse once I am a dying vegetable at age 47. This weekend it has been about not being able to breathe. But that is a combination of asthma and anxiety. Because basically there is a gradual shut down happening that involves my heart, lungs, brain, and all my innards with literally no exceptions. And I want to keep myself from being like "it's always something," because really I have such a freaking easy life now. I mean it could not be more easy and yet sometimes I still wish I was in the hospital getting more attention. But that is in fact for real reasons and having a feeling of a panic attack for almost a whole week is actually a rather severe health problem.

But there are a lot of people with that level of mental illness problems right now who don't know how to find a doctor. So anyway, what was I saying. I am saying I am having a nice day. I chose to list out my understanding of persecution feelings because I keep wanting to explain all this to people. Like people don't understand. But I can tell everyone is mad when I complain. Like the consensus is that I have enough to go on not to complain. And I kind of think that is true but sometimes I feel like based on the information I have, people don't know what they are doing by not allowing my normal participation in society. And now for a fifth career loss, and that career was an accumulation of four other mastered skills and in a category of competent mass communication that yes absolutely would have had a societal impact and should have. But people think that selling books is like winning the lottery so I am deluded. Okay fine. There is no need for me to keep sqwawking about it. Tell me the truth, should I have started that paragraph about the walker and stayed happy about how I drank some coffee? Like to say, I drank two coffees today and took a walk. But does that cut the mustard for the conspiracy who helped me so much and watches helplessly as nothing happens each time I publish another book? Like nothing at all? That I sit around and drink coffee as if I have never worked? Honestly I am a little bit stumped on that one. Really, do you guys want me to not complain? To say this is fine? It is such a deep tragedy that I search my life and soul to try to figure out if I offended God in some way. Like what did I do for God to waste this kind of life and work. And I think the answer is that it isn't God, and he hates some people who are reading this.

What Next

Well everyone, this is a post for my new positive post blog, which isn't some kind of philosophical positive thinking blog, but just a blog where I don't complain. And I have actual good news to share, which is that I finished my imaginary mice series a few days ago, and I think after the poetry book I am also working on, I might finish up with my main writing works. I think I might think of myself as finished with what I have to say, other than maybe one or two collections for any random poems I think of later on. I have always thought that's not how it works, and I would be a poet for life. And I guess I am, but I think for some reason I feel like I have said enough for my share of books and unexpectedly decided that the mice series is also finished. So maybe I will still post little comedy videos or something, but I think I have written what I have written. I thought of it just now because of having trouble charging my phone, which has been the case with every iphone I owned after the iphone 4, and I might be done with apple products too. Maybe I will surprise myself and still use that technology since I am used to it, but I might not. I might let myself be an out of touch fuddy duddy who watches the world go to hell in a handcart, or online amazon shopping cart. That is all I will say, before this post starts to match my old blog, which might still have room for how I feel about apple scams.

Visit my new blog of positive posts…

Hi everyone, I have started a new blog where I say
happy things that are going well.

If you want to read some funny books, I wrote 40 books
and published them on amazon. It is mostly poetry and
I think young people would like a lot of the writing:

refriedbean.com

The books are also a cheerful resource for people with
depression, and I myself have survived mental illness
for about twenty-five years.

If you want to learn some things about Christianity, a lot
of my books share some jokes that also have valuable
information and prayer ideas. Mostly the concept is that
God will love anyone and you can ask for any blessings
you would ever want and be surprised. I feel that my
problems in life have obscured this some for readers
and that is why I am trying to start a new blog.

I found a huge bear at the grocery store

hi everyone,

I found this bear next to the dumpster at the grocery store and brought it home as a decoration. It seems plenty clean and I am excited about it.

Thanks, everyone, who read my blogs at any time. This blog went through a phase of rant posts and I am now starting over with a new blog to say things I am happy about. I suspect it could take on a sarcastic tone sometimes but I feel that I would rather not be too much of a complainer when I have enough food and safety and am not being tortured behind a cash register.

So thanks everyone, have a great day.

Monkeypox Ice Box Pie Recipe

Just joking everyone, it is not a monkeypox pie but a kool-aid pie that I just made. It is yummy and my new favorite recipe. There are three links below to some of my favorite youtube cooks. They have a lot of videos. It is Hillbilly Kitchen, which has a lot of cool easy recipes like two ingredient fudge. And Preppy Kitchen, which is really like kind of technically advanced sometime but still clean and clear to understand. And then the one that really gets me every time is Camirra's Kitchen, which I almost can't believe the creativity and skill, and most of all the yumminess of the food and the consistently huge amount and variety of flavorings, like spices, and other yummy ingredients. And just the random stuff the person knows. So anyway, I watch other cooks videos on there too sometimes, so maybe I will post more sometime. But these guys are definitely some of my favorites and I have tried a few recipes myself.

Favorite YouTube Cooking Show Channels:

Hillbilly Kitchen:
https://www.youtube.com/watch?v=m1z1r1OcoQQ&t=608s

Camirra's Kitchen:
https://www.youtube.com/watch?v=Xc7cXJaMkao

Preppy Kitchen:
https://www.youtube.com/watch?v=pnfPzermXxk

A Rap That I Made Up for Fun

Canto I

My name is Refried Bean and I am writing this nice rap
Explaining my mistakes and other people's bogus crap

I think I'll say a lot of stuff and tell it how it is
And share all what I have to say like I'm some kind of whiz

You see a rhyme that's not that good but that's what I am doing
To just have fun and say the reasons why you won't be suing.

So what does that refer to well I'll tell you in this rhyme
And then you might read other stuff at some good other time.

Well mainly I would like to say that Satan's evil plans
Will always backfire in a way that takes away his fans.

He never wins but we will see that things are all for good
And justice happens all the time the way it really should.

You might get tired of this whole verse before it's even done.
But I am keeping writing even after it's not fun.

I'll say the punchline early on which has to do with pain
And what went wrong within my life and drove us all insane.

Satan chose to hide behind my mom and family.
But that did not work out for him as you will prob-ly see.

It only meant I felt some love from where the evil came.
And so my faithful patience catapulted God to fame.

But it is like that anyhow and God won't lose his place
And he will share his love with anyone who seeks his face.

Well what did that just mean I'll say that I don't really know.
But as I said before that's what I do in this rap show.

So anyway as I was saying, Satan is so bad.
And that is why a lot of people made me really mad.

But I was taught to love and pray and do the best I can.
And other people helped me know that Jesus was a man.

You see how that was kind of forced, like writing that's not great
But I will write this anyway to talk about my fate.

And honestly I start to think that books like Dante's works
Might be like this and written with a lot of lazy quirks.

But just because it rhymed then people read it anyway
And now they know a lot of stuff that God was nice to say.

And it is quite a claim to call your writing prophecy,
But all I write is that I say the truth that speaks to me.

So anyway as I was saying I have worked so hard
To do what I think seems the best in my own heart to guard.

I do not know what that just meant but I will say I've sinned,
A lot and every day but I have also learned to mend.

And I've been there for other people sad or hungry too.
And showed up every day to life to do what I can do.

I worked a job for twelve whole years when it seemed really bad,
And people tried to hurt my mind and make me really sad.

So then I moved to New York City, hoping to enjoy
A happy life away from all the villains who annoy

But evil found me here as well and tried to strike me dead
With all disturbance you could find that hurts my very head.

However I will choose to stay alive and pray so much
And sometimes hide away from people where they cannot touch.

And now I take a break to buy some milk from down the street.
But I'll return to tell the tale of God's great meet and greet.

Canto 2

So now I'm back to my apartment with some milk and food.
And this part of the rhyme describes how people are so rude.

I almost can't walk down the street or go to any store
Because of all the street harassment, racism, and more.

The people block the groce-er-ees and hurt me in the line,
And breathe on me on purpose just to act like it is fine.

A motorcycler rides upon the sidewalk I am on
When all the streets are clear and he just wants me on the lawn.

A night club guy would block my path with all his nasty gang
Until I had to call the cops and beg to buy some Tang.

My facebook friends are friendlier but even some of them
Like politics so much that they just spit on me with phlegm.

This is how you rap and rhyme and think along the way
It's easy finding all examples, things of what to say.

So as I wrote before I just can't stand all the abuse
And if I listed all of it I'd be a Dr. Seuss.

And while I have to say that asking God for love is nice
Forgiving people is a dream I have instead of vice.

But what I feel has happened is that better things are blocked
So I can't do what's really right and stores aren't fairly stocked.

And that is what will make me question why I'm even born,
And what should best be done if all I'm meant to do is mourn.

And really is it mourning or some lesser kind of rage
That means all the solutions are ideas from off the page?

My question then is violence the answer for these woes?
And does our God expect us to destroy these nasty foes?

Well I don't have a gun and I believe in sacrifice
And if the immigrants are hurt it won't be me who's ICE.

So as you see this rap took a direction of surprise,
Because it's really anyone who has to now be wise.

And solve the problems government is paid to handle all
And find a tough conundrum for each nine eleven call.

Well I don't think my life should be too simple fun and great
If other people suffer and their children haven't ate.

But I know crime and hate won't pay and that is what I see
So fighting is a moral ground that seems not bad to me.

However I will also try to keep on praying lots
For all the people and their children needing tater tots.

Because I know conspiracies have gotten in the game
And thought of crazy things to do to help with God's great name.

In hopes that those who torture us will find out what they need.
And live their lives in heaven thanks to Jesus' saving deed.

Which happened on the cross in times that must've been much worse
And God chose our forgiveness over every single curse

So anyway the other thing I feel compelled to say
Is wow the rhymes on radios are better every day

Than this cheap list of things that bother me so much in life,
The rappers also write a lot about their problem strife.

But I have never listened much because I like some tunes
That focus more on melodies and folky misty moons.

So now you say moon river must be like a song you love
Well yes that's true and also Hallelujah holy dove.

Which wasn't on the radio til people such as me
would play it on our DJ show while kicked in our own knee.

I'm joking, it was not the knee, it was my very face
And not a margined group but God and all his human race.

So don't expect to think the punishment is not for you
Unless you take salvation that is offered by a Jew.

Canto 3

Well as I said before I just am writing as I go,
And thinking of a little rap that ends this poet show.

Because I thought I might as well decide to make this stop,
Like all the rabbits in my books who rest from each great hop.

And maybe I will write some poems if something hits my mind,
But really that's the problem as I'm sure that you will find.

My brain is deconstructing and my heart is beating slow,
And all my health is not so good as you must now well know.

So soon I won't control myself when feeling bad or good
And other people only help me do the things I should.

With forty books complete I'll say that might be quite enough,
And I freaked out a lot when life was really not that tough.

I ate a lot of food and I made jokes with lots of friends,
And most of us aren't famous by the time our life soon ends.

So why should I complain too much in all my later work
When what the people wanted was some jokes or what's berserk.

But did they really want that and will they still want it now?
Or were they all just lying and they want to eat some cow.

That's hamburgers and ketchup and a milkshake melting fast
When I worked hard to give them something nice that all could last.

But as I try to give my books to any reader kind,
I see the clock is ticking fast and life will soon unwind.

And I'll be on my dying bed not knowing who I am
And hopefully I'll still be with a person like a yam.

Well that was really in-ter-esting, what does it all mean?
I really do not know but I have tried to keep it clean.

So all my writing might be passed along to people's kids,
Despite the fact that no one offered cash or any bids

When I first tried to sell my books with such a growing need
To flee the people with the cash who hurt me with their feed.

So do you mean your mother or your friends or company?
Or was it all the social workers saving lives for free?

Or all the people in the street or in the news so bad
Or in the ads you see online to make you buy each fad.

You see how rhymes like this can be quite fun to read and write,
And how a person might learn how to talk like this each night.

For all their life and never say a free verse once again,
And that is like the people who have hurt me with their sin.

Our whole wide world is now presented with amounts of choice
To listen to the bad TV or hear our God's own voice.

Who says he'll take us back and make the bad things not come true,
Like when the people hate me and then say they're going to sue.

Instead of reading any book that could have made them laugh,
And taught the people how to eat their fruit and half and half.

A joke with jokes and jokes some more could really bless the earth,
Instead the people mock us all with cruelty as mirth.

So this was how the poets wrote in all the days gone by,
Except their poems were better or at least in their own eye.

And if you think that all of this is all I know to do,
Then I would say the one to question more is really you.

Because I spent a lot more thought and time on other stuff,
But all the people seem to think that nothing is enough.

Which brings us back to how it was in my important days
Of getting out of college just to learn the grown-up ways

With everyone against me and deciding just to waste
A friendly brain that thinks a lot and smartly handles haste.

Well now we see what's lost and if this book goes in the trash,
Then you can all expect to try again at heaven's bash.

Refried Bean lives in the Bronx, NY
at Waters Place, near a Stop and Shop.
Refried writes funny poetry and stories
for kids and adults who want some
easy and fun but interesting ideas
that can suddenly later on
sprout into a magic thought forest.